Volcanic Eruptions

Peachtree

ANN O. SQUIRE

Children's Press®
An Imprint of Scholastic Inc.

Content Consultant
William Barnart, PhD
Assistant Professor
Department of Earth and Environmental Sciences
University of Iowa
Iowa City, Iowa

Library of Congress Cataloging-in-Publication Data
Squire, Ann O., author.
Volcanic eruptions / by Ann O. Squire.
   pages cm. — (A true book)
Includes bibliographical references and index.
ISBN 978-0-531-22299-7 (library binding : alk. paper) — ISBN 978-0-531-22515-8 (pbk. : alk. paper)
1. Volcanoes—Juvenile literature. I. Title. II. Series: True book.
QE521.3.S68 2016
551.21—dc23   2015022172

All rights reserved. Published in 2016 by Children's Press, an imprint of Scholastic Inc.
Printed in China 62
SCHOLASTIC, CHILDREN'S PRESS, A TRUE BOOK™, and associated logos are trademarks and/or registered trademarks of Scholastic Inc.
1 2 3 4 5 6 7 8 9 10 R 25 24 23 22 21 20 19 18 17 16

**Front cover: Mount Kilauea erupts in Hawaii
Back cover: A researcher watches lava flow
from Mauna Loa in Hawaii**

Find the Truth!

Everything you are about to read is true *except* for one of the sentences on this page.

Which one is **TRUE**?

T or F   Volcanoes often form at the edges of Earth's tectonic plates.

T or F   The volcanoes found in the Hawaiian Islands produce the world's most explosive eruptions.

Find the answers in this book.

Contents

THE BIG TRUTH!

Frozen in Time

3 Anatomy of a Volcano

Escaping gas is one sign that
a volcano is active.

A Hawaiian volcano erupts in a curtain of fire.

In areas threatened by volcanoes,
advance planning can save lives.

Before its eruption in 1980, Mount St. Helens had a much different shape than it does today.

CHAPTER 1

What on Earth?

For thousands of years, Mount St. Helens in Washington was one of the most beautiful peaks in the Cascades. This mountain range stretches from British Columbia to Northern California. Like many other mountains in the Cascades, Mount St. Helens is a volcano. In early 1980, it rose steeply to a high peak. Its summit and sides were covered with snow and glaciers. However, the mountain would soon change.

This volcano's steep slopes are made up of layers of ash and debris.

Early Warnings

Seismologists had set up a network of devices to monitor earthquake activity in the Cascades. In March 1980, the devices reported an earthquake beneath Mount St. Helens. Over the next few days, there were many more earthquakes. On March 27, steam and ash erupted from the volcano. The eruption blew out a 230-foot-wide (70 meters) crater at the mountain's summit.

Spectators watch Mount St. Helens erupt from a safe distance in 1980.

The Mount St. Helens bulge grew by more than 6 feet (2 m) every day!

A Growing Bulge

The eruption created two long cracks that extended almost 1 mile (1.6 kilometers) down the volcano's sides. Over the next few weeks, more steam eruptions and earthquakes occurred. This caused the part of the mountain between the cracks to start bulging out. By early May, the mountain had expanded outward by more than 300 feet (91 m).

A woman camps safely in the area surrounding Mount St. Helens in 1997, well after the volcano erupted.

A Dangerous Camping Trip

Many people in the area were tempted to take a closer look at the changes happening on the mountain. Michael Moore of Longview, Washington, decided to take his family camping near Mount St. Helens. They pitched their tent 13 miles (21 km) northwest of the mountain. They thought this would be a safe distance. But like many people, the Moores underestimated the incredible power of the volcano.

Landslide!

On the morning of May 18, another earthquake shook Mount St. Helens. Although it was not a very violent quake, it was strong enough to dislodge the bulging part of the mountain. The entire north side broke away, creating a gigantic landslide. The landslide also released pressure that had been building up inside the volcano. The result was a massive explosion that sent a column of gas into the sky and rained ash over 11 states.

Mount St. Helens released an astounding amount of ash into the sky when it erupted.

A Lucky Escape

At their campsite, the Moores heard a loud rumbling and saw ash shoot into the air. Michael Moore started to snap photos, but the sky soon darkened. He realized he and his family were in danger. Looking around, he spotted an abandoned shack. They rushed inside as black clouds of ash rolled in, flattening trees and sparking a lightning storm. When the cloud finally passed, everything for miles around was covered in a thick layer of ash.

Ash clouds spread into nearby towns in Washington.

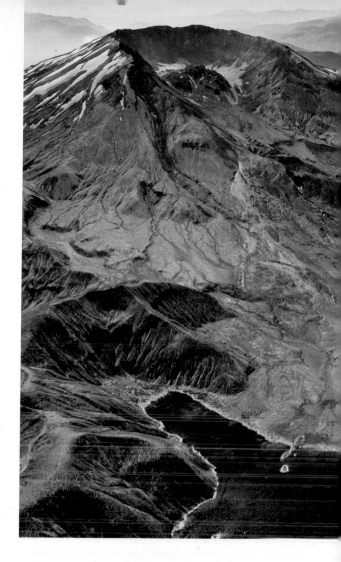

The eruption in 1980 destroyed the peak of Mount St. Helens, leaving a huge crater.

Ash and dust filled the air, making it hard for people to breathe. Fallen trees blocked the way back to the Moores' car. After spending a night in the woods, the family was rescued by helicopter. Though they went through a terrifying experience, the Moores were among the lucky ones. The Mount St. Helens eruption killed 57 people. If a large town or city had been nearby, the death toll would have been much higher.

An erupting volcano can be a beautiful sight when viewed from a safe distance.

Volcanic ash and dust limits visibility and damages airplane engines. This makes air travel difficult.

CHAPTER 2

Up From Underground

Most people would describe a volcano as a steep mountain with a crater at the top. They would say that when the volcano erupts, hot **lava** bubbles up from deep within the earth and flows down its sides. Some volcanoes do look and act that way. However, there are many different types of volcanoes. In fact, almost any place where **magma** from inside Earth makes its way to the outside can be considered a volcano.

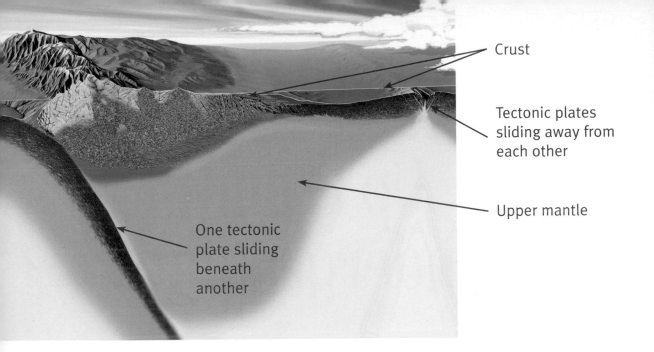

Crust

Tectonic plates sliding away from each other

Upper mantle

One tectonic plate sliding beneath another

A Layered Planet

To understand how and why volcanoes form, it helps to know a bit about the **geology** of our planet. Earth's hard outer shell is called the lithosphere. The lithosphere is made up of a top layer of rocky crust and a denser lower layer. It is not smooth and solid. Like a cracked eggshell, it is broken up into a number of large chunks called tectonic plates. Volcanoes often form along cracks where the plates are moving toward or away from one another.

Tectonic Plate Movement

Beneath the lithosphere is a layer called the asthenosphere. It is also made of rock. However, this rock is hotter and softer than the upper layer. The tectonic plates shift and move above the soft layer underneath. If you've ever cracked an egg, you know that the liquid inside seeps out along the cracks. In the same way, hot material from underground sometimes escapes at places where the tectonic plates meet.

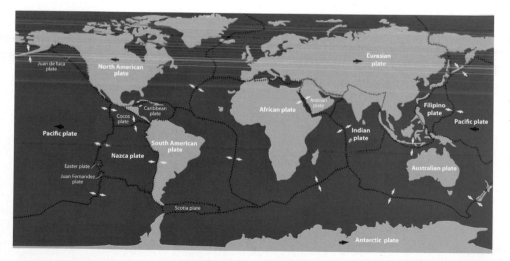

Volcanoes are most common in areas where the edges of tectonic plates (shown with red lines) touch.

Spreading Out

Spreading center volcanism happens when two tectonic plates move apart. This typically occurs on the ocean floor. As plates move away from each other, hot material from underground rises to fill in the space between them. The material cools to form rocky ridges along the ocean floor. Underwater volcanoes of this type do not erupt violently. This is because the melted rock is not under pressure. Instead, it leaks out slowly and adds to Earth's crust as it cools.

Lava seeps out

Plates move away from each other

Spreading center volcanism is not usually as explosive as other types of volcanic activity.

Earth's tectonic plates are constantly moving.

Subduction zone volcanism can produce incredibly explosive eruptions.

Eruption

One plate moves underneath the other

Moving In

When Earth's tectonic plates move toward each other, one plate slides underneath the other. This forms what is called a subduction zone. Heat from deep within the planet releases water from the bottom plate. This lowers the melting point of rocks in the top plate and allows them to melt. Magma forces its way through to the surface and erupts. Because the magma is under pressure, eruptions of these **stratovolcanoes** are often violent.

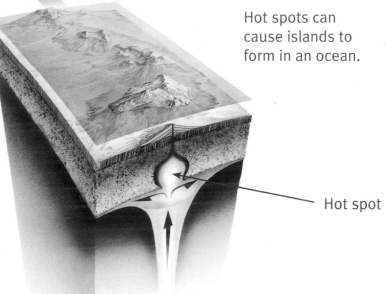

Hot spots can cause islands to form in an ocean.

Hot spot

Hot Spot Volcanism

Not all volcanoes form where tectonic plates meet. They can also occur in the middle of a plate. Scientists believe this is caused by large columns of magma called plumes. As a plume's magma rises, it creates a "hot spot." Above it, a volcano forms. Earth's tectonic plates are always in motion, however, and the plume stays still. What happens as the plate moves over the hot spot?

As a plate moves, a hot spot volcano will gradually move past the plume and become less active. A new volcano will develop some distance away, near the plume of magma. This eventually results in a string of inactive volcanoes with an active volcano at the end. The Hawaiian Islands are a good example of this. Of Hawaii's eight major volcanoes, seven are inactive. The Hawaiian hot spot currently lies under the "Big Island" of Hawaii. That island has several active volcanoes.

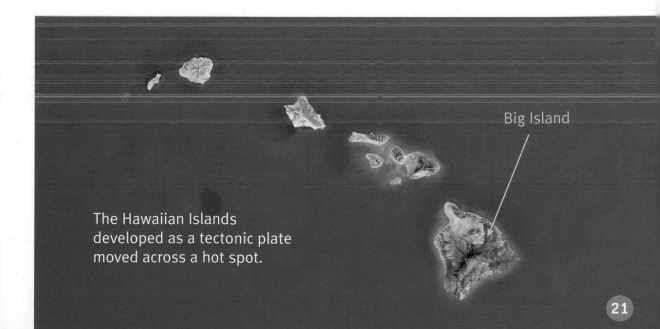

Big Island

The Hawaiian Islands developed as a tectonic plate moved across a hot spot.

A Different Look

Hawaii's volcanoes look very different from Mount St. Helens. Instead of rising to a peak, the Hawaiian volcanoes are smooth and rounded. This is because they erupt differently. Instead of exploding quickly, Hawaii's **shield volcanoes** usually produce a slow, steady flow of lava. As a result, they are typically the least dangerous type of volcanoes. However, they can sometimes erupt violently and suddenly.

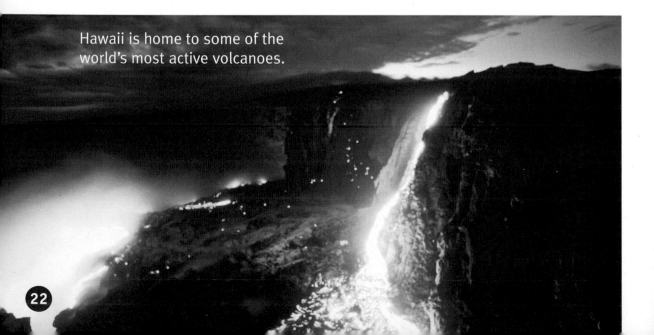

Hawaii is home to some of the world's most active volcanoes.

The Yellowstone Supervolcano

Yellowstone National Park in Wyoming lies above a large hot spot. Earth's crust is very thick in this area. As a result, large amounts of magma build up underground with no way to escape. When the pressure becomes too great, this **supervolcano** erupts violently. Yellowstone's last big eruption was 640,000 years ago. Another one could happen at any time. Some scientists believe that Yellowstone will one day explode with a force 1,000 times more powerful than the Mount St. Helens eruption.

Yellowstone's natural beauty may one day be disrupted by a major eruption.

Frozen in Time

No one expected Mount Vesuvius to erupt in 79 CE. There had been earthquakes, but there was no written record of any eruption before then. The mountain just sat quietly in the Bay of Naples in Italy. However, on August 24, 79 CE, Vesuvius exploded.

First, earthquakes caused buildings in nearby Pompeii and Herculaneum to collapse. Then a column of ash, rock, and gas shot more than 12 miles (20 km) into the air. As the cloud spread, ash and rock rained down on surrounding towns.

At about midnight, the ash column collapsed. Rock and gas raced down the volcano at 450 miles per hour (700 kph). At 750 degrees Fahrenheit (400 degrees Celsius), this pyroclastic flow caused rapid destruction. People caught in its wake died instantly. More pyroclastic flows followed.

The eruption lasted for about 25 hours. By then, it had wiped out Pompeii, Herculaneum, and other nearby towns. They remained buried for nearly 1,700 years. When explorers happened upon Pompeii in 1748, they found a marvel. The ash had preserved everything it covered. People, animals, and objects were left where they had fallen that fateful day in 79.

Some volcanoes have extremely large magma chambers.

Magma chamber

CHAPTER 3

Anatomy of a Volcano

Whether it's a Hawaiian shield volcano or the explosive Mount St. Helens, all volcanoes have a similar structure below the surface. Underneath every volcano is at least one magma chamber. This is where partially molten rock collects and pushes its way toward the surface. Magma, ash, and gas escape to the surface through a main channel or cracks along the sides of the volcano.

The word for "volcano" comes from Vulcan, the Roman god of fire.

Magma Rising

Why does magma rise to the surface rather than remain underground? As magma heats up, it becomes lighter than the rock surrounding it. This causes it to rise upward. As the magma moves, bubbles of gas form in it and make it even lighter. The weight of the magma and the amount of trapped gas help determine what kind of eruption will occur. Other factors include the thickness of the ground above the magma and whether the volcano is underwater.

This photo inside the crater of Ethiopia's Erta Ale volcano shows lava bubbling up as gas is released from underground.

Slow-moving lava flows form rock on the surface as they cool.

Hawaiian Eruptions

Eruptions of shield volcanoes like those found in Hawaii are often less explosive than other eruptions. One reason for this is the small amount of gas in the magma coming to the surface. This amount of gas can easily escape, because the magma is runny and thin, like honey. As a result, very little pressure builds up underground. This allows the lava to flow out smoothly and gradually.

Lava often launches high into the air during a Plinian eruption.

Plinian Eruptions

At the other end of the spectrum are violent explosions known as Plinian eruptions. These can occur when a volcano contains magma with lots of gas trapped inside. This magma is thick and solid, almost like peanut butter. It doesn't flow easily, so the gas cannot escape. Eventually, the pressure of the gas and magma becomes dangerously high. When that happens, the volcano explodes and spews ash and hot gases into the sky.

Ring of Fire

About 90 percent of all earthquakes and 75 percent of all active volcanoes occur in a ring around the Pacific Ocean. This violent line of activity is called the Ring of Fire. It lies along the edges of tectonic plates beneath the ocean floor. In all, the ring is about 25,000 miles (40,233 km) long. It stretches up from New Zealand through Asia, past Russia and Alaska, and down the west coast of North and South America.

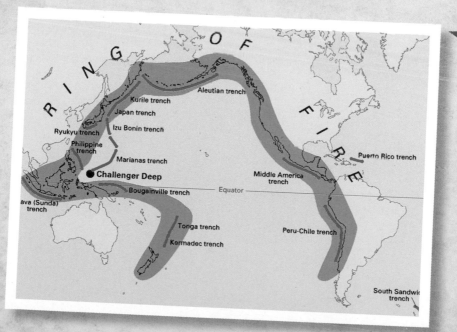

Because of its eruption, Mount Tambora was reduced to being 9,354 feet (2,851 m) tall.

Mount Tambora may look peaceful most of the time, but its 1815 eruption was deadly.

CHAPTER 4

Volcanoes That Changed the World

Some of the world's most famous eruptions were explosive. In 1815, the most powerful volcanic eruption in recorded history occurred at Mount Tambora in Indonesia. The eruption blew the top third off the 14,000-foot (4,267 m) mountain. Thousands of people died as pyroclastic flows ran into nearby farms and villages. Ash fell across Southeast Asia, blanketing farmland and destroying crops. Many people who survived the eruption died of starvation and disease later.

A pyroclastic flow can be one of the most dangerous parts of an eruption.

Widespread Disaster

Wind picked up the dust released by Mount Tambora and carried it around the globe for over a year. High in the sky, it blocked the sunlight. Earth's average temperature dropped by more than 5°F (3°C). The effects were felt as far away as Europe and North America. The unusually cold weather killed crops, put farmers out of business, and created serious food shortages. As a result, 1816 became known as "The Year Without a Summer."

Krakatau

Sixty-eight years later, another Indonesian volcano made history. On August 27, 1883, the volcanic island of Krakatau erupted. The explosion was heard in Australia, nearly 2,800 miles (4,506 km) away. Superheated steam formed as seawater poured into the magma chamber. Pyroclastic flows traveled in all directions for 25 miles (40 km). In addition, the top of Krakatau slid into the sea. This displaced a huge amount of water, creating a **tsunami**. The wave wiped out some nearby islands completely.

Ash can be so plentiful that it buries homes and other buildings as it settles.

Child of Krakatau

After the eruption, only one-third of the island of Krakatau remained. The space where the volcano had been became covered by water. Things were calm for a while. But not long after, a new volcano began to emerge from the depths. Anak Krakatau (Child of Krakatau) first appeared in 1927 in the space where the old volcano had been. Anak Krakatau is very active. It erupts frequently as it continues to grow.

Timeline of Major Volcanic Eruptions

1815

Mount Tambora erupts, leading to the Year Without a Summer the following year.

1883

Krakatau erupts. Thousands of people die in the resulting tsunami and pyroclastic flows.

Mount Pinatubo

One of the most powerful 20th-century eruptions occurred in 1991 in the Philippines. Mount Pinatubo had been quiet for 500 years. Tens of thousands of people lived on its slopes and in the valleys below. Despite its long silence, however, scientists monitored the volcano. They noticed warning signs, such as earthquakes, that meant a possible eruption. As a result, officials evacuated everyone within 15 miles (24 km) before Pinatubo erupted on June 15. Many lives were saved.

1980
Mount St. Helens erupts, raining ash over 11 states.

1991
Mount Pinatubo erupts for the first time in 500 years.

A geologist studies deposits from past eruptions near Alaska's Mount Redoubt volcano.

Geologists study Earth's top layers to learn about past volcanic eruptions.

CHAPTER 5

Surviving Eruptions

Researchers have developed many ways to forecast possible future eruptions. One method is studying past eruptions. For recent events, scientists review eyewitness accounts, photos, and videos. They also look at prehistoric eruptions. How? Volcanoes change the landscape. Geologists see traces of explosions, ash, and lava by looking at an area's bedrock. They learn about when, where, and how violently a volcano erupted. This tells the scientists what future eruptions from the same volcano might be like.

Keeping Watch

Scientists also keep a close eye on a volcano's current activity. They use seismographs to watch for the earthquakes that indicate magma is on the move. Other instruments track swelling in a volcano's slopes. When gases and magma collect inside a volcano, it causes the sides of the volcano to bulge out. Instruments also monitor the amount and makeup of volcanic gases. An increase in sulfur dioxide is a good sign an eruption might be on its way.

A geologist in Cape Verde measures the gases escaping from a volcano on Fogo Island.

People in cities near active volcanoes, such as those in the shadow of Popcatépetl, in Mexico, have learned to be prepared for the unexpected.

Limitations

There is no way, however, to perfectly predict a volcanic eruption. Experts can estimate when an eruption is likely to occur. But they cannot know exactly when it will take place. Sometimes, an eruption doesn't occur at all. Magma might move and cause earthquakes, but cool without erupting. In addition, many volcanoes have long periods between eruptions. This dormancy may be so extended that people think the volcano is extinct (no longer producing lava). Nearby residents may be unprepared when the volcano finally erupts.

Evacuation routes are planned and marked before an eruption takes place.

Staying Prepared

It's important to be prepared for volcanic eruptions, especially since they are unpredictable. Officials plan evacuation routes and decide when and what areas to evacuate. Residents should also have plans in place. They need to know how to meet up with family members or friends and how they'll travel to evacuate. Sometimes officials ask residents to stay and take shelter. For these events, residents should know the location of a safe place and how to get there.

Destruction to Creation

Volcanoes are destructive, but they also have positive effects. They can create new land, such as islands. Eruptions have also supplied most of the water on Earth, from the oceans to the moisture in the air we breathe. In addition, volcanic ash often contains important nutrients that make soil incredibly fertile. Volcanoes can even provide energy to power plants, which turn that energy into electricity. Good or bad, volcanoes are a dangerous and awe-inspiring part of nature. ★

Volcanic ash has made Java's farmland very fertile.

Number of active volcanoes on Earth today:
About 1,500

Number of people who live within 60 miles
(90 km) of an active volcano: 800 million

Percent of Earth's active volcanoes located
along the Ring of Fire: 75

Percent of volcanic eruptions that occur
underwater: 75

Number of volcanoes erupting somewhere in
the world at any given moment: 20

Height of Olympus Mons on the planet Mars,
the tallest volcano in the solar system: 17 mi.
(27 km)

Percent of Earth's surface that was created by
volcanic activity: 80

Did you find the truth?

Volcanoes often form at the edges
of Earth's tectonic plates.

The volcanoes found in the
Hawaiian Islands produce the
world's most explosive eruptions.

Resources

Books

Furgang, Kathy. *Everything Volcanoes and Earthquakes*. Washington, DC: National Geographic, 2013.

Meister, Cari. *Volcanoes*. Minneapolis: Jump!, Inc., 2016.

Rusch, Elizabeth. *Eruption! Volcanoes and the Science of Saving Lives*. Boston: Houghton Mifflin Harcourt, 2013.

Visit this Scholastic Web site for more information on volcanic eruptions:
www.factsfornow.scholastic.com
Enter the keywords **Volcanic Eruptions**

Important Words

geology — (jee-AH-luh-jee) the study of Earth's physical structure, especially its layers of soil and rock

lava — (LAH-vuh) the hot, liquid rock that pours out of a volcano when it erupts

magma — (MAG-muh) melted rock found beneath Earth's surface that becomes lava when it flows out of volcanoes

pyroclastic flow — (pye-roh-KLAS-tik FLO) a fast-moving current of hot gas and rock that travels down the sides of volcanoes after certain types of eruptions

seismologists — (size-MAH-luh-jists) scientists who specialize in the study of earthquakes

shield volcanoes — (SHEELD vahl-KAY-nohz) broad volcanoes built up from the repeated nonexplosive eruption of lava to form low domes or shields

stratovolcanoes — (stra-tuh-vahl-KAY-nohz) large, steep volcanoes built up of alternating layers of lava and ash or cinders

supervolcano — (SOO-pur-vahl-kay-noh) a volcano that erupts much more forcefully than most

tsunami — (tsoo-NAH-mee) a very large, destructive surge of water caused by an underwater disturbance

Index

Page numbers in **bold** indicate illustrations.

About the Author

Ann O. Squire is a psychologist and an animal behaviorist. Before becoming a writer, she studied the behavior of rats, tropical fish in the Caribbean, and electric fish from central Africa. Her favorite part of being a writer is the chance to learn as much as she can about all sorts of topics. In addition to the *Extreme Earth* books, Dr. Squire has written about many different animals, from lemmings to leopards and cicadas to cheetahs. She lives in Long Island City, New York.